AGRICULTURAL ENGINEERING
AND Feeding the Future

Crabtree Publishing Company

www.crabtreebooks.com

Anne Rooney

Crabtree Publishing Company

www.crabtreebooks.com

Author: Anne Rooney

**Publishing plan research
   and development:** Reagan Miller

Photo research: James Nixon

Editors: Paul Humphrey, James Nixon,
   Kathy Middleton

Consultant: Carolyn De Cristofano, M.Ed.
   STEM consultant, Professional Development Director
   of Engineering is Elementary (2005-2008)

Proofreader: Wendy Scavuzzo

Layout: sprout.uk.com

Cover design and logo: Margaret Amy Salter

**Production coordinator and prepress
   technician:** Margaret Amy Salter

Print coordinator: Margaret Amy Salter

Written and produced for Crabtree Publishing Company
by Discovery Books

Photographs:
Alamy: pp. 15 bottom (epa european pressphoto agency
   b.v.), 16 (dpa picture alliance), 17 top (REDA & CO srl),
   28 (Islandstock).
Bigstock: pp. 4 (Makaule), 6 (sherjaca), 7 bottom (Ralko),
   8 (bfoxfoto), 9 bottom (Erik deGraaf), 11 bottom (leaf),
   13 top (teekaygee), 14 (endomotion), 15 top (Paha_L),
   17 bottom (Leonid Ikan), 18 (budabar), 19 top (Phillip
   Minnis), 19 bottom (Trevui), 22 (lfstewart), 23 bottom
   (Geert Weggen), 24 (Gamjai), 27 (moritorus), 29 top
   (underworld1), 29 bottom (Alens).
Getty Images: pp. 7 top (The Asahi Shimbun), 9 top
   (KOEN SUYKMIDDENMEER/AFP), 11 top (Time Life
   Pictures/Mansell), 21 bottom (Koichi Kamoshida/
   Stringer), 23 top (Buyenlarge).
Robotics: pp. 20 and 21 top (Domenico Longo & Giovanni
   Muscato).
Shutterstock: Cover: top right (muratart), background
   (Iakov Filimonov), bottom right (Dennis Albert
   Richardson)
Wikimedia: Cover middle right (Public Domain) pp. 5
   (U.S. National Archives and Records Administration),
   10, 12 (NOAA George E. Marsh Album), 13 bottom
   (U.S. Fish and Wildlife Service), 25 top (NASA), 25
   bottom (U.S. Library of Congress).

Library and Archives Canada Cataloguing in Publication

Rooney, Anne, author
    Agricultural engineering and feeding the future /
Anne Rooney.

(Engineering in action)
Includes index.
Issued in print and electronic formats.
ISBN 978-0-7787-7504-1 (bound).--
ISBN 978-0-7787-7525-6 (paperback).--
ISBN 978-1-4271-9996-6 (pdf).--
ISBN 978-1-4271-9992-8 (html)

    1. Agricultural engineering--Juvenile literature. I. Title. II.
Series: Engineering in action (St. Catharines, Ont.)

S675.25.R66 2015   j631.3   C2015-903387-X
                                          C2015-903388-8

Library of Congress Cataloging-in-Publication Data

Rooney, Anne, author.
  Agricultural engineering and feeding the future / Anne Rooney.
    pages cm. -- (Engineering in action)
  Includes index.
  ISBN 978-0-7787-7504-1 (reinforced library binding) --
ISBN 978-0-7787-7525-6 (pbk.) --
ISBN 978-1-4271-9996-6 (electronic pdf) --
ISBN 978-1-4271-9992-8 (electronic html)
  1. Agricultural engineering--Juvenile literature. 2. Food supply--
Juvenile literature. I. Title. II. Series: Engineering in action.

  S675.25.R66 2016
  630--dc23
                              2015021745

Crabtree Publishing Company

www.crabtreebooks.com   1-800-387-7650

Printed in Canada/082015/BF20150630

Published in Canada
Crabtree Publishing
616 Welland Ave.
St. Catharines, ON
L2M 5V6

Published in the United States
Crabtree Publishing
PMB 59051
350 Fifth Avenue, 59th Floor
New York, New York 10118

Published in the United Kingdom
Crabtree Publishing
Maritime House
Basin Road North, Hove
BN41 1WR

Published in Australia
Crabtree Publishing
3 Charles Street
Coburg North
VIC, 3058

CONTENTS

WHAT IS AGRICULTURAL ENGINEERING?

Providing a secure food supply to everyone on the planet is one of the greatest challenges facing the world. **Climate change** and an increasing population mean that in some areas people struggle to grow enough food to survive. Agricultural engineers and farmers are leading the effort to meet these challenges. **Agriculture** is not concerned only with food. It also involves the **cultivation** of, or methods of growing, living things for food, fuel, or materials. The practice of agricultural methods is called farming.

Agricultural engineering aims to develop **sustainable** methods of farming, which means methods that will not damage the environment. Engineers develop mechanical and electronic technologies to make agriculture more efficient—that is, to produce more while using fewer **resources**. Other types of engineering are often involved, including mechanical, electrical, computer, chemical, food, and **genetic engineering**.

Agricultural engineers have to take many issues into account, including plant and animal health, and climate change. They must also consider ethical issues—whether actions are morally right or wrong. It means weighing different points of view in matters such as how we treat animals or affect the environment.

Agricultural engineers work to design farm machinery, develop processes for treating crops, and help to protect the soil.

EIGHT STEPS TO SUCCESS

Agricultural engineers follow an eight-step process to perfect their designs (see right). It covers designing, building, testing, and improving technologies.

Engineering and science

Science and engineering are closely linked. Scientists investigate the world, trying to discover the rules by which natural processes work. Engineers apply the findings of science to make useful technologies. An agricultural scientist might investigate how a plant takes **nutrients** from the soil. An agricultural engineer would use that information to develop ways of delivering nutrients to plants. Agricultural engineering works with many types of science, including computing, robotics, chemistry, environmental science, **botany**, **zoology**, **ecology**, and **nutrition**.

GEORGE WASHINGTON CARVER

Agricultural engineering technologies include processes. George Washington Carver was an inventor and botanist, born a slave in Diamond Grove, Missouri, around 1864. After slavery was abolished, he became a farmer for a while. He went on to study botany at college, and later became head of the agriculture department of the Tuskegee Institute in Alabama. He encouraged and taught farmers to rotate crops, growing cotton one year, then switching to sweet potatoes or peanuts the next year. Both these crops replace nitrogen, taken from the soil by growing cotton. This makes the soil fertile enough to grow cotton again.

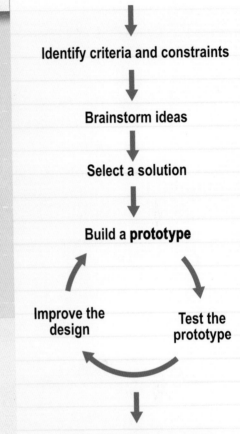

Steps in the design process

Define the problem

↓

Identify criteria and constraints

↓

Brainstorm ideas

↓

Select a solution

↓

Build a **prototype**

↓ (Test the prototype)

Test the prototype

Improve the design

(Build a prototype ↑)

↓

Communicate the solution

George Washington Carver was a pioneer in soil management.

WHAT IS A BIOSYSTEM?

Agricultural engineering is often called agricultural and biosystems engineering. A **biosystem** is a complex network of living organisms—plants, animals, and **microbes**—that interact with each other. Organisms live together, feed off each other, and affect each other in this network, which is called a system. A biosystem is the living part of an **ecosystem**, in which organisms interact with the physical environment. Agricultural engineers need a full understanding of how biosystems and ecosystems work so that they don't accidentally or dangerously disrupt them.

Pests and diseases are a major problem for farming. Pests such as insects attack crops, and some microbes cause disease in animals and plants. For much of the 20th century, farmers used chemical **pesticides** and medicines to tackle pests and diseases when they struck, or even before to prevent them. Using harsh chemicals can disrupt biosystems and harm the soil, water, and farming products.

Cattle and the grass they eat are part of a biosystem. Microbes in the cows' guts and insects in the soil are also part of this biosystem.

IPM: Modern agriculture relies on Integrated Pest Management (IPM) systems to try to prevent problems. Instead of relying on chemical **interventions**, farmers choose plants that have been bred to resist disease. They monitor conditions in the field and act early if anything goes wrong. They make use of natural relationships between organisms to control conditions. For example, **predators** can be introduced to reduce insect pests. They use mechanical or robotic **hoes** to remove weeds instead of using chemicals, and use **herbicides** and pesticides only where they are needed.

A robot designed to weed paddy fields where rice is grown is tested in Japan.

COMPANION PLANTING

Some plants produce chemicals that certain pests don't like. Planting these among crops can deter pests. For example, growing carrots and leeks together protects carrots from carrot fly and leeks from leek moth. The insects don't like the smell of the other vegetable.

Colorado potato beetles can ruin potato crops if not controlled. Farmers can spread a fungus that kills the beetles without using chemicals.

THE FOUR PESTS CAMPAIGN

A program introduced in China in 1958 aimed to kill four pests: rats, flies, mosquitoes, and sparrows (birds that ate crops). Killing birds backfired disastrously. It led to a plague of insects that did even more damage than the birds. Killing the birds left no predators to eat the insects. The result of failing to understand the biosystem led to widespread starvation. The result was the Great Chinese Famine, which caused 20 million deaths.

HOW THINGS GROW

Agricultural engineers need to understand the science behind growing plants and animals, including what they need to grow and the energy flow involved.

All energy flows from the Sun. It gets into the biosystem through plants, which are called primary producers. Plants take energy directly from the Sun through **photosynthesis** to make their own food. To grow, plants need energy from the Sun; water; air; and nutrients from the soil. Animals are called secondary producers because they take energy from food, not directly from the Sun. They need water and air, as well as energy and nutrients from food to grow. Some animals get their energy from eating plants, which get their energy from the Sun. Other animals get their energy from eating other animals.

Making farming efficient: Agricultural engineers help work out efficient means of production. They develop technologies and methods for:

- protecting or improving the soil, and irrigating, or watering, crops
- using **fertilizers to** deliver the chemical nutrients needed by plants
- sowing, weeding, fertilizing, and harvesting crops, and for housing, caring for, and processing **livestock**
- combating pests and diseases by using pesticides for plants and medication for animals

Newly planted corn is irrigated with a sprinkler system in Oregon.

A farmer raising livestock, such as sheep or cattle, has to give attention to the **fodder** the animals eat and to their well-being. It takes more land and energy to farm livestock than to grow crops, because livestock farming also needs land for growing fodder. Beef from cattle provides food containing only one tenth as much energy as the cattle have taken in from fodder. This is because the cattle use most of their energy from food in other life processes and activities. Farming meat is much less efficient in terms of producing food energy for humans than farming plants such as wheat and rice.

Vast glasshouses in Holland supply light 24 hours a day to plants. Carbon dioxide waste from factories is pumped in to speed up photosynthesis to grow larger, sweeter peppers and tomatoes.

The engineering solutions in this rice field in Indonesia are simple: baskets and a walkway between flooded paddies.

A GLOBAL ISSUE

People farm all over the world on different types of land. In some areas of the world, people have less money and less technology than in other areas. Agricultural engineers must take into account the resources available to the farmers they work with and for. They must design solutions to farming problems that are affordable and easy to put into place with the tools and procedures the farmers already have.

IMPROVING FARMING THROUGH HISTORY

People have been doing some form of agricultural engineering since the days of the very first farms. The earliest farmers designed simple tools such as hoes, spades, **scythes**, and **plows**. They built **irrigation** and drainage systems to increase yield (the amount of crop produced). They selectively bred animals and crops, choosing those which produced plentiful milk or thick wool. They came up with the idea of fencing to protect crops from being eaten by animals and protect livestock from predators such as wolves.

A revolution

The agricultural revolution in the 1700s brought rapid changes in farming. These changes helped to feed a growing population. It began in Britain, but soon spread. Farmers added new crops, including turnips and clover. Crops were grown in rotation, changing the crop in a field over a three- or four-year cycle. This prevented damage to the soil, which happens when a crop takes the same nutrients out of the soil year after year. Growing turnips helped control weeds. Turnips grow in straight rows and farmers could hoe between the rows without damaging the turnips. Clover grown for fodder helps put nitrogen back into the soil. New machinery was introduced, some of it powered by steam. Waterlogged marshland was drained and used for farming.

JETHRO TULL, 1674-1741

Born in England in 1674, Jethro Tull trained to be a lawyer. When he became ill, he searched everywhere for a cure. As he traveled, he observed different agricultural practices. On his return to England, he devoted himself to modernizing farming. He is considered to be the first person to take a scientific approach to agriculture—the first modern agricultural engineer. Most famously, he developed a horse-drawn hoe, and a mechanical **seed drill**. The seed drill mechanized the sowing of crops by making holes in the soil in evenly spaced rows, dropping seeds into the holes, and covering them with earth. The hoe also made it easy to remove weeds between rows. Both improved yields and saved work.

Using Jethro Tull's seed drill, a farm worker could quickly, easily, and evenly sow seeds at the right depth, and even cover them with soil.

Less work: Farming used to employ much of the population, but agricultural engineering has changed that by automating tasks that previously took a lot of manual work. In 1900, 38 percent of the American workforce was employed in farming, but by 2000 it was only 3 percent with no drop in food production.

The next big change came in the 1950s. Automation, which means using machines to do things automatically, made it easier for farmers to manage much larger areas of land. Some farms became huge. They were run using machinery that took over for farm workers. Farmers also began using large quantities of chemicals such as pesticides, herbicides, fertilizers, and **antibiotics** for livestock.

Motorized harvesters can quickly harvest even the vast fields of the North American prairies.

LEARNING FROM PAST MISTAKES

Today, agricultural engineers are greatly concerned with issues such as sustainability, animal welfare, and **organic** farming. Animal welfare means that livestock must be kept in suitable conditions so they are healthy. Organic farming is farming without using industrially-manufactured chemical pesticides, fertilizers, and herbicides. Past mistakes have taught us that agricultural practices can have a dangerous impact on the environment if all consequences are not carefully considered first.

The Dust Bowl

In the 1930s, American and Canadian farmers suffered terrible consequences from bad farming methods combined with drought. The result was the devastation of a large area of farmland, which became known as the Dust Bowl. Topsoil, which is the rich soil plants need to grow, was loosened by too much plowing. It was stripped away by winds that ripped across fields with no hedges or trees to stop it. Dust storms whirled millions of tons of black dirt through the air, leaving about 500 million acres (202 million ha) useless for growing crops. Agricultural engineers quickly turned their attention to protecting the soil—an issue that is now central to farming practices. The U.S. government paid farmers to plant trees as windbreaks and use methods that prevent soil **erosion**.

Thick black dust covered the landscape during the Dust Bowl years of the 1930s.

Insect killers

A different type of disaster began in the 1940s, but this time the worst effects were avoided by quick action. The widespread use of an effective insecticide, called DDT, began to affect biosystems by killing birds. In the 1950s, most countries banned the use of DDT in farming. Bird populations recovered. Now agricultural engineers look for ways of reducing herbicide and pesticide use. Whatever is used is tested first for its impact on biosystems.

DDT built up in the bodies of birds of prey, such as eagles, harming them.

RACHEL CARSON

Rachel Carson was a biologist and writer who investigated the effects of DDT and other pesticides. Her book Silent Spring, published in 1962, sparked the move toward sustainable farming and the reduced use of chemicals. Agricultural engineers began to develop new, more environmentally responsible ways of growing and protecting crops.

WORKING IN AGRICULTURAL ENGINEERING

Agricultural engineers can work on farms, in university research departments, machine factories, government departments, and aid organizations. People follow different paths into agricultural engineering. Some people finish a degree in agricultural engineering, but many train first in agriculture or other relevant areas of engineering. There are high-level jobs in design and advising on new farming methods, and entry-level jobs in maintaining and monitoring equipment.

Skills: Agricultural engineers need a good understanding of the science behind agriculture. It's also important to be able to work with others and, for some types of work, to enjoy being outdoors. Creativity is also a valuable asset. It helps you find new ways to solve problems—ways not tried before.

A researcher examines a new type of corn in a field. The worker's protective clothing prevents any contamination of the crop samples.

There is work for agricultural engineers in widely different areas including:

- Farm machinery, such as tractors and combine harvesters, milking machinery, housing for livestock, and machines for processing and storing products such as eggs, grain, wool, and cotton.

At most dairy farms, much of the milking process involves using automated machinery.

- Robotics is a field concerned with carrying out tasks automatically, such as monitoring the condition of crops and animals, controlling automated harvesting, and destroying weeds. Work in this field requires skills in computer engineering and robotics.

- Resource management covers a broad range of work. It can include projects that also involve chemical and **civil engineering**. It might be concerned with soil preservation, animal welfare, water use, or developing sustainable farming practices.

RESTORING THE SOIL

An engineer investigates damage to farmland after a tsunami in Japan in 2011.

Agricultural engineers working with an international charity advised farmers in Indonesia on how to restore their fields after a **tsunami** flooded their land with seawater carrying debris and **sediment**. The engineers explained which types of sediment had to be removed, and how to do it without causing more damage. Peat-rich sediment was fertile and could be left to mix with the soil, but thick deposits of clay and sandy sediment had to be removed. The correct action also depended on the type of underlying soil and the crops the farmers wanted to grow. Growing rice in irrigated fields helped to remove salt from the soil left by the seawater. Other crops, such as peanuts and vegetables, could be grown afterward.

THE ENGINEERING PROCESS

The first stage in tackling a problem in agricultural engineering is to identify the problem and state it clearly. Next, engineers set out the criteria and conditions the solution must meet. We can see how this works by looking at a project to design a machine to pick artichokes.

The problem: Artichokes are an important crop on the island of Sicily in Italy, providing a livelihood for many small farmers. The artichoke is a type of thistle. The edible part is the flower bud, which must be harvested before it opens. Traditionally, artichokes are cut by hand one at a time. Harvesting absorbs about 20 percent of the cost of growing artichokes. Could it be mechanized? Two Italian agricultural engineers, Domenico Longo and Giovanni Muscato, worked with an artichoke farmer to develop a robot for harvesting artichokes.

Cutting artichokes with a knife in the hot sun is not a comfortable job—but a robot wouldn't mind!

Criteria: Experienced harvesters can cut by hand an average of 6.25 artichokes per minute. Any solution must match this speed. It must identify artichokes that are ready to harvest, cut each artichoke, and collect it without damaging it or other artichokes.

Constraints: It must cost less to build and run the robot than it would cost to pay workers to harvest artichokes by hand, year after year. The robot must be narrower than the space between the rows of artichokes.

Artichoke are shown being harvested by hand in Sicily, Italy.

This tractor is pulling a modern seed drill.

SLOW IMPROVEMENTS

Many farming practices have evolved over centuries, with improvements carried out in stages by different people. Change often starts when people notice a problem or disadvantage with the way things are done.

Sowing seeds by hand is wasteful and results in a low yield. The problem is to find a more efficient way, so that less seed falls where it cannot grow.

The earliest solution was a tube that makes a hole in the soil and drops seeds into it, first used in Babylon around 3,500 years ago. Farmers in China used a modified version 1,300 years later. It had several tubes side by side to plant seeds in rows.

Jethro Tull's seed drill (see page 11) was similar but had added disks to pull the soil over the seeds, protecting them and greatly reducing waste.

Modern seed drills pulled by tractors separate the seeds, sending them for planting at the right rate to achieve the best spacing. Because they cut into the soil, the farmer does not need to plow the field first. Plowing disturbs the soil and can make soil erosion more likely.

BRAINSTORMING AND CHOOSING IDEAS

Brainstorming is a creative approach to problem-solving. A team of scientists and engineers come up with lots of different ideas, thinking in new ways. Engineers then evaluate the approaches they have come up with and decide which fit the requirements and criteria best.

Agricultural engineers often work closely with farmers and visit farms to discuss new ideas.

Brainstorming the artichoke harvest:
The Italian engineers working to improve artichoke harvesting thought at first they could make a machine that cuts ripe artichokes individually, like human harvesters do. But brainstorming suggested a second possibility—perhaps they could cut down whole groups of plants.

Choosing an approach: The engineers thought that both approaches seemed promising. They could not tell which approach would be best, so they decided they would take both ideas to the next stage. They were not building anything yet, so the investment was low. Each design would use a small electric vehicle that moved between the rows of plants.

One design, called a selective harvester, cut only ripe artichokes it had "selected." It had two cutting arms and used an artificial vision system to identify the artichokes ready for harvesting. It would cut a ripe artichoke with one arm, and cut another with the second arm at the same time if it was within reach. It then moved on to the next ripe artichoke. Harvested artichokes were collected on a platform.

The other design, called a mass harvester, cut every artichoke above a certain height in a "mass" cutting. It had moving blades which could be set by the operator to suit the crop. This meant it also cut lots of leaves, which had to be removed later. The harvested artichokes and vegetation fell into large crates.

Robotic harvesting is well advanced in some areas of farming. This tractor has a harvester attached to pick grapes in Australia.

RICE OR SHRIMP?

The Mekong Delta in Vietnam is an important rice-growing area, but is increasingly affected by **encroaching** salt water. The Vietnamese government has constructed embankments and gates to control the flow of water, but the problem is getting worse. Agricultural engineers have come up with a number of different solutions for keeping the land useful for farming:

• **tributary** dams, which feed fresh water into the Mekong River during the dry season, flushing out saltwater

• growing strains of rice with higher salt tolerance

• farming shrimp instead; the land would still be productive, but without struggling against environmental change.

Rice farmers could face ruin if salt water from flooding invades their land.

TESTING AND PROTOTYPES

The engineers tested their designs for an artichoke harvester by using computer software to simulate the robots' behavior. This prevented the need to build expensive machinery as prototypes for testing, and did not risk a crop, which would be costly to the farmer if it didn't work.

Software prototypes: The two different machines were designed, then computer models were made of each one. Engineers used photographs of a real field of ripe artichokes to create a virtual, or computer-simulated, field. They tested each design in a simulated harvest.

The robotic vision system for the selective harvester analyzed an image of part of the field from above, looking for dense patches which represent ripe artichokes. If a clump was dense enough, the onboard computer treated it as a ripe artichoke and instruct the cutting arm to harvest it. Otherwise, it ignored it. In the areas the harvester identified as having ripe artichokes, engineers could go to the real field and count (a) correct identifications of ripe artichokes (b) incorrect identification (dense leaf clusters that were not artichokes), and (c) missed artichokes.

The selective harvester has arms with grippers to carefully pick individual artichokes.

The mass harvester cut all vegetation over a certain height. To test its efficiency, engineers modeled how many artichokes were below the cutting height and so were missed, and how many unripe artichokes were wasted by being harvested too early. Human harvesters then worked on the real field, marking as damaged any unripe artichokes that would have been picked by the mass harvester, or low-growing artichokes that would have been missed.

The mass harvester has sharp cutters that slice through whole plants.

SOME THINGS FAIL

Harvested crops must be transported without damage. Watermelons are difficult to transport efficiently since spheres do not stack well. They must not knock into each other in transit or they will be damaged. Instead of looking at just packaging solutions, imaginative engineers thought of changing the watermelons themselves. They designed a metal frame to force them to grow into cubes. Tests with prototypes found that the watermelons filled the frame too soon, before they were ripe. Farmers increased the price of the square watermelons and sold them as decorative items! The crop was not wasted, but the problem was not solved.

A watermelon grown in the shape of a cube looks good, but is not tasty.

EVALUATING AND IMPROVING THE DESIGN

After testing a physical or virtual prototype, engineers evaluate the results. How well did the design solve the problem? What was good and what was bad? How could it be improved?

Evaluating methods: The engineers evaluated the artichoke-harvesting robots by comparing the software harvests with the real harvest. They found that the mass harvester was almost ten times faster than the selective harvester. Unfortunately, though, it damaged a lot of artichokes and harvested many that were unripe. It could not meet farmers' requirements. The selective harvester had a low rate of damage but was too slow. With further development, it might be possible to improve it sufficiently. The research is ongoing: the next stage will be to build a physical prototype and test it with real artichokes. Artichoke planting patterns could also be adjusted to make it easier for a harvester to work.

Changing the way artichokes are planted could help engineers develop a better harvester.

Trade-offs

Often, engineers working on new designs have to accept trade-offs: accepting a compromise on one aspect of a design so they can meet other requirements. In designing an artichoke harvester, engineers and farmers had to consider the trade-off between the speed of harvesting and a reduced saleable crop because of damage or wastage.

BINDING AND REAPING

When small-grain plants such as wheat or rice are harvested, the stalks are tied into bundles—a time-consuming process. In 1872, American Charles Withington invented a **reaper**-binder machine to cut and tie sheaves of harvested grain with wire. Its limitations showed up in use. Bits of wire broke off and ended up in the grain and were even eaten by cattle fed the crop. In 1879, William Deering, an American businessman, began selling an improved version of Withington's design, using twine instead of wire.

A mechanized reaper-binder made life much easier for farmers.

People who grow soft fruits in their gardens or on patios have to protect them against hungry birds.

Activity: Many people grow foods such as beans and strawberries in their gardens. Birds like to eat these crops, too. Choose a garden or patio crop and design a way of protecting it from birds. Will you drive birds away or make a physical barrier around the crop? Remember—the crop must remain easy to water and harvest. Your design must be weatherproof, cheap, and easy to make. If possible, create and test your design. Can you suggest improvements?

23

REFINING AND SHARING THE PROJECT

Feedback from testing helps engineers to refine the solution. Sometimes, further, unexpected problems set new challenges. These can spark new developments. Sharing discoveries by publishing articles or giving presentations means others can develop an idea further, or it might be relevant to other engineers' projects.

Water and air

Hydroponics is a way of growing crops without soil. It can use either just water with dissolved nutrients, or the plants can be rooted in a solid soil-substitute, called a substrate, but still get all their nutrients from the solution. The substrate does not provide nourishment, but anchors the plants' roots.

Batavia, a type of lettuce, is grown hydroponically in a large greenhouse.

People first tried hydroponics in the 1600s, when they had little understanding of plant nutrition or chemistry. They found that the cleaner the water was, the less well the plants grew, but they did not know why. In 1929, American William Gericke began promoting the method, hoping that hydroponics could be developed commercially to produce food in areas with poor soil. He published his findings in a book, and other agricultural engineers and scientists began to work on it. One early success was using hydroponics to grow vegetables on Wake Island in the Pacific Ocean. It is a rocky, volcanic island with no soil and no other way of growing food.

Agricultural engineers looked for other methods that could be used with different crops. They developed aeroponics (growing plants in the air) and fogponics (growing plants in a mist of water vapor).

When astronauts finally visit Mars, they might grow their own food using aeroponics.

Only images of Cyrus McCormick survive. Because Jo Anderson was a slave, it is likely his photograph was never taken.

CYRUS MCCORMICK AND JO ANDERSON

The first commercially successful automated reaper was made in 1831. Like many inventions in agricultural engineering, it was the result of work by many people, but was finished and popularized by Cyrus McCormick and his slave, Jo Anderson. An American, McCormick was the son of an inventor who had tried for years to develop a mechanical harvesting machine based on earlier designs. McCormick and Anderson perfected the design after the death of McCormick's father. The machine made harvesting quick and easy, and allowed farmers to farm more and more land in the west of North America.

DESIGN CHALLENGE

Could you be a good agricultural engineer? Find out by trying this challenge.

All plants need just the right amount of water. With too little, they dry out and wither—too much makes their roots rot.

Develop a system for watering a raised bed of vegetables. Try it out on a small scale. You will need:

- plastic food trays, bottles, and boxes

- rubber tubing, straws, long balloons, or other items you could use as tubes

- soil or compost, and stones

- seeds of fast-growing plants, such as mustard or cress

1: Identify the problem: A farmer can't spend all day pouring water onto plants from a hose or watering can, so an effective watering system is essential. Your design must supply water at the right rate to keep the plants healthy. The constraints are the items you have available to work with (listed), and the needs of the type of seeds you choose. For example, some seeds need to be covered, or be kept warm, but others do not.

2: Research the problem: Engineers find it useful to do some research to find out more about the science that backs up their work. Find out about how water flows, the requirements of plants, and drainage and water **retention** in soil to help with your own project. You could try some experiments, as well as read about the topics. Someone who grows plants in containers might be able to give you advice, too. The expertise of others is a valuable resource.

3: Brainstorm possible solutions: Draw up some designs using different methods of storing and delivering water. Label your plans clearly so that it's obvious how the design will work. For example, you might use a plastic bottle to hold the water, and balloons or tubes to deliver it to soil in a plastic box or tray.

4: Select a solution: Pick the design that you think will work best to meet the criteria, working with the constraints of the materials you have and the needs of your seeds.

5: Build a prototype: Build your prototype following the plan. If you find that anything doesn't work as you expected or that you need to use different materials, keep notes of what you have changed and why. The way a design develops is important information that can help with future designs.

6: Test and evaluate your solution: You will need to plant the seeds and run your system for about a week to find out how well it works. Look for signs of the soil being too dry or too soggy. It should feel damp but not have water oozing out if you press it. Is it evenly moist over the surface? How often does the water reservoir need to be refilled? Can you see any problems with your design? How might you address them?

7: Communicate the solution: Make a poster or write a report to explain your design, the problem it addresses, and how it works. Ask other people to look at it and give you any suggestions they can think of for improvements.

8: Refine your design: Can you improve the design to work better with the same type of seeds? How could you adapt it to suit plants that need more or less water than the plants you have tried?

Many people grow houseplants. Could you modify your system to water houseplants while the owner is away on vacation?

INTO THE FUTURE

Climate change and increased need for housing due to growing populations are reducing the amount of the world's farmable land. The challenge for the 21st century is to grow more food using less land. The benefits of making farming more efficient are better yields and enabling farmers to manage the same amount of land with fewer staff.

New foods

Agricultural engineers are investigating structures and methods for growing new types of food. One is mycoprotein, made from a type of fungus grown in towers 130–164 feet (40–50 meters) tall. The fungus takes only about six hours to grow using a mix of nutrients and sugar. It is then extracted and the mycoprotein is processed to become a substitute for meat.

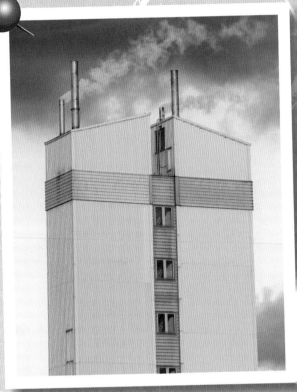

This mycoprotein factory can produce four batches of mycoprotein each day.

Better crops: One way agricultural engineers hope to increase food production globally is by creating genetically modified (GM) crops. These are made by taking DNA (genetic material) from one plant and adding it to another to give it new or better characteristics. GM crops can be made so that they are protected against pests, grow better, and keep for longer after harvesting. One GM crop being investigated is called C4 rice. This has been changed to photosynthesize more efficiently. Using it, farmers in developing countries could increase their rice yield by 50 percent using the same amount of land. As with any new scientific method, scientists have been testing over the past few decades for any harmful effects from GM crops on animals, consumers, and the environment.

Hands-off farming

Driverless tractors guided by satellite systems in space, robotic shepherds, and flying robotic drones that check weed control from the air are all in development as agricultural engineers help to automate tasks for farmers. Automated harvesters will increasingly monitor and report on the yield of crops, giving farmers vital information. Remote, or distant, management of machinery by smartphone means farmers can even go on vacation and still manage their farms!

Farmers and engineers in the future will always be trying to find ways to increase the yields of crops, such as these bananas.

ROBOTIC SHEEPDOG

Engineers at Swansea University, Wales, are developing software that could be used to control a robot to herd sheep. At the moment, dogs are used to drive sheep where the farmer wants them to go. Engineers began by recording the exact movements of working sheepdogs and sheep. By looking carefully at the movement patterns, they figured out how sheepdogs herd sheep. They found that they first move the sheep together into a group, then move the whole group. Software to control the robot copies the way the sheepdogs work. When the software is ready, the engineers can begin work on a robotic sheepdog to try out with real sheep. Robotic sheepdogs could work endlessly without tiring.

Sheepdogs herd sheep using methods that can be analyzed and recreated in software and robotics.

LEARNING MORE

BOOKS

Bingham, Jane. *Producing Dairy and Eggs* (The Technology of Farming). Raintree, 2013.

Gibbard, Stuart, et al. *Tractor: The Definitive Visual History*. Dorling Kindersley, 2015.

Mason, Helen. *Agricultural Inventions: At the Top of the Field* (Inventions That Shaped the Modern World). Crabtree Publishing, 2013.

McManus, Lori. *Producing Fruits* (The Technology of Farming). Raintree, 2013.

Morrison, Heather S. *Inventors of Food and Agriculture Technology* (Designing Engineering Solutions). Cavendish Square Publishing, 2015.

Owen, Ruth. *Growing and Eating Green: Careers in Farming, Producing, and Marketing Food* (Green-Collar Careers). Crabtree Publishing, 2010

Owings, Lisa. *Sustainable Agriculture* (Innovative Technologies). Abdo Publishing, 2013.

ONLINE

www.deere.co.uk/en_US/corporate/ our_company/fans_visitors/kids/john_ deere_in_action.page?
Videos of different types of farm machinery in action.

12most.com/2012/03/12/advanced- agricultural-technologies/
Twelve recent developments in agricultural engineering, from tractors that talk to each other to ear tags that monitor the health of cows.

www.livinghistoryfarm.org/ farminginthe30s/farminginthe1930s. html
The history of the Dust Bowl and its impact on farming. This site has histories of different eras of farming in American history, including information about machinery used in each.

www.explainthatstuff.com/ howcombineharvesterswork.html
How combine harvesters work; search this site for information on how other types of farm machinery work.

www.agclassroom.org/gan/timeline/ farm_tech.htm
A timeline of agricultural engineering inventions in North America.

GLOSSARY

agriculture Raising animals and plants to produce food, materials (such as wool), or fuel

antibiotics Medicines that kill a type of microbe, called bacteria; Antibiotics are used to prevent or cure bacterial infections in animals and humans.

biosystem A network of plants and animals that live together

botany The scientific study of plants

civil engineering Engineering that deals with the built environment, including roads, bridges, buildings, and other structures

climate change A long-term shift in the planet's weather patterns or average temperatures

cultivation Growing and caring for plants

ecology The scientific study of how living things interact with the environment

ecosystem A system involving the interactions between a community of living organisms in a particular area

encroaching Creeping in

erosion Removal of soil from the land by flowing water or wind

fertilizer A substance that provides nutrients to plants to help them grow

fodder Feed for livestock, especially dried, chopped hay

genetic engineering Changing animals or plants by working with their genes (which carry inherited characteristics)

herbicide A chemical used to kill weeds

hoe A tool used to loosen weeds by disturbing the soil around their roots

intervention A measure to interrupt a process

irrigation Providing water to crops in a controlled way

livestock Farm animals

microbe A living thing too small to see with the naked eye

nutrients Chemicals needed by a living organism to live and grow

nutrition The science or study that deals with food and the substances necessary for life and growth

organic Describing crops grown without using artificial pesticides, herbicides, fertilizers, and medicines

pesticide Any chemical used to kill pests such as insects or mites that harm crops

photosynthesis The process by which plants make food (sugar) from sunlight, carbon dioxide, and water

plow A tool for breaking up the soil to make it easier to plant seeds

predator Animal that preys on and eats another animal

prototype A first working model of an invention used for testing

reaper A machine that cuts down and harvests grain

resources Supplies available for use

retention Keeping or holding onto something

scythe A tool with a curved blade and a long handle, used for cutting grain crops and grass

sediment Solid matter that has settled or been left behind after being carried by a liquid, such as soil collecting in a waterway

seed drill Equipment for making holes in the soil and depositing seeds into the holes

sustainable Describing the ability to grow food now and in the future using methods that do not harm the environment

tributary A river or stream leading into a main waterway

tsunami A rapid flood of seawater that washes over the land in a series of huge waves, causing destruction

zoology The study of animals

INDEX